Spiritual Warfare and You

INSPIRED BY CHRIST JESUS
AND THE HOLY SPIRIT

Debra Kay Houston Wong,
Evangelist Minister

ISBN 978-1-0980-7816-4 (paperback)
ISBN 978-1-0980-7817-1 (hardcover)
ISBN 978-1-0980-7818-8 (digital)

Christian Faith Publishing, Inc.
832 Park Avenue
Meadville, PA 16335
www.christianfaithpublishing.com

Printed in the United States of America

To my family, my grandmother Carrie Mae Walker Dukes, my mother, Mary Larkin Houston, and my father, Woodrow Wilson Houston. My children, Gregory Lee Wong Jr., Erica Marie Wong Simms Subramanian, and Yvette Marie Wong. My grandchildren, Ronald Eugene Simms III and Ryan Eugene Simms.

CONTENTS

PREFACE

This book was written to express the urgency that the Lord Christ Jesus is coming back soon for his bride, the church.

A SERVANT OF CHRIST JESUS

I am Debra Kay Houston Wong, an Evangelist minister and a true servant of Christ Jesus. My mission in life is to praise, worship, and to obey the Word of God. I began my walk in Christ Jesus, in a Christian Baptist family. I accepted Christ Jesus as my Lord and Savior at the age of nine years old and was baptized like Christ Jesus in total water submersion at Macedonia Baptist Church, March 1964 in Los Angeles, California. I completed a two-year Bible study with Bible prophecy by mail. I raised my three children, Gregory Wong Jr., Erica Wong Simms Subramanian, and Yvette Wong, and two grandchildren, Ronald Simms III and Ryan Simms, in the Word of God as Christians. I graduated in 2015 from Southern California School of Ministry in Inglewood, California.

My Christian lifework has been as an adult and youth Sunday school teacher for over forty years, a church missionary leader for adults and youth groups for over twenty years, and a street outreach organizer for years at three different churches. I am a LVN case manager, a computer trainer, and an evangelist minister directly called by Christ Jesus.

INTRODUCTION

Hello, people of the world. I want you to know that we live in a temporary physical world so that we can make our personal decision to accept Christ Jesus as our Lord and Savior, to be with him for an eternity or to reject him and be dammed to the everlasting lake of fire that was prepared for the devil, aka Satan, and the fallen angels, aka demons.

God the Father (Yahweh), God the Son, Christ Jesus (Yeshua), and the Holy Spirit had a plan before the foundation of the world that Christian believers would be reconciled back to God in fellowship through the shedding of blood (crucifixion) of Christ Jesus.

> According as he hath chosen us in him before the foundation of the world, that we should be holy and without blame before him in love. (Ephesians 1:4 KJV)

John 14:6 (KJV) says there is only one way to be saved from the wrath of God, "Jesus saith unto him, I am the way, the truth, and the life: no man cometh unto the Father, but by me."

There is no jumping over Christ Jesus to get to God the Father.

Jesus is the answer to all of life and death issues.

CHAPTER 1

The Beginning of Spiritual Warfare in Heaven

In the beginning, God created the heaven and the earth.

—Genesis 1:1 (KJV)

And there was war in heaven: Michael and his angels fought against the dragon; and the dragon fought and his angels, And prevailed not; neither was their place found any more in heaven. And the great dragon was cast out, that old serpent, called the Devil, and Satan, which deceiveth the whole world: he was cast out into the earth, and his angels were cast out with him. And I heard a loud voice saying in heaven, now is come salvation, and strength, and the kingdom of our God, and the power of his Christ: for the accuser of our brethren is cast down, which accused them before our God day and night. And they overcame him by the blood of the Lamb, and by the word of their testimony; and they loved not their lives unto the death.

—Revelation 12:7–12 (KJV)

God created Lucifer. Lucifer, aka Satan, in his ignorance, forgot that he is a creation of God that can never be greater than the Creator. The power that he has was given to him by God. The angels that followed him were of a rebellious spirit, and so they sided with Satan. However, God had mercy on them. He could have destroyed them, but he allowed them to be cast down to the earth.

CHAPTER 2

The Beginning of Spiritual Warfare on Earth

When Evil Fell to Earth

Therefore. rejoice, ye heavens, and ye that dwell in them. Woe to the inhabiters of the earth and of the seal for the devil is come down unto you, having great wrath, because he knoweth that he hath but a short time. And when the dragon saw that he was cast unto the earth, he persecuted the woman which brought forth the man child. And the dragon was wroth with the woman, and went to make war with the remnant of her seed, which keep the commandments of God, and have the testimony of Jesus Christ.

—Revelation 12:12-13, 17 (KJV)

God Command to Adam

But of the tree of the knowledge of good and evil, thou shalt not eat of it: for in the day that thou eatest thereof thou shalt surely die.

—Genesis 2:17 (KJV)

The Serpent

Now the serpent was more subtil than any beast of the field, which the LORD God had made. And he said unto the woman, Yea, hath God said, Ye shall not eat of every tree of the garden? And the woman said unto the serpent, we may eat of the fruit of the trees of the garden: but of the fruit of the tree which is in the midst of the garden, God hath said, Ye shall not eat of it, neither shall ye touch it, lest ye die. And the serpent said unto the woman, Ye shall not surely die: for God doth know that in the day ye eat thereof, then your eyes shall be opened, and ye shall be as gods, knowing good and evil.

—Genesis 3:1–5 (KJV)

The Serpent

And when the woman saw that the tree was good for food, and that it was pleasant to the eyes, and a tree to be desired to make one wise, she took of the fruit thereof, and did eat, and gave also unto her husband with her; and he did eat. And the eyes of them both were opened, and they knew that they were naked; and they sewed fig leaves together, and made themselves aprons. And they heard the voice of the LORD God walking in the garden in the cool of the day: and Adam and his wife hid themselves from the presence of the LORD God amongst the trees of the garden.

Genesis 3:6-8 (KJV)

There was no talk of death, until the day that Adam bit the apple, then mankind started dying physically and spiritually. Adam was held accountable because God had given him the command not to eat the fruit from the tree of Knowledge, not Eve. Adam was standing alongside of Eve when the devil convinced Eve to eat the fruit from tree of knowledge. He did not reject the devil's lies, but instead he bit the apple in order to please Eve more than God. Adam was disobedient to God

CHAPTER 3

∽◈∾

The Consequences of Sin on Earth

Adam and Eve Expulsion from the Garden of Eden

And the Lord God called unto Adam, and said unto him, where art thou? And he said, I heard thy voice in the garden, and I was afraid, because I was naked; and I hid myself. And he said, who told thee that thou wast naked? Hast thou eaten of the tree, whereof I commanded thee that thou shouldest not eat? And the man said, the woman whom thou gavest to be with me, she gave me of the tree, and I did eat. And the Lord God said unto the woman, what is this that thou hast done? And the woman said, the serpent beguiled me, and I did eat. And the Lord God said unto the serpent, Because thou hast done this, thou art cursed above all cattle, and above every beast of the field; upon thy belly shalt thou go, and dust shalt thou eat all the days of thy life: And I will put enmity between thee and the woman, and between thy seed and her seed; it shall bruise thy head, and thou shalt bruise his heel. Unto the woman he said, I will greatly multiply thy sorrow and thy conception; in sorrow, thou shalt bring forth children; and thy desire shall be to thy husband, and he shall rule over thee. And unto Adam he said, because thou hast hearkened unto the voice of thy wife, and hast eaten of the tree, of which I commanded thee, saying, Thou shalt not eat of it: cursed is the ground for thy sake; in sorrow shalt thou eat of it all the days of thy life.

—Genesis 3:9–17 (KJV)

After Adam and Eve disobeyed God, their life would never be the same. Eve and the snake would forever be enemies. Eve and womankind would have great sorrow in bringing forth children, and Adam and mankind would have to work for his food all the days of his life. Willful disobedience to God brings about punishment.

Everyone is accountable for their own action, and the decision they make to please Christ Jesus or to please the world will decide their eternal destination.

CHAPTER 4

Salvation Only Comes through Christ Jesus

For God so loved the world, that he gave his only begotten Son, that whosoever believeth in him should not perish, but have everlasting life.

—John 3:16 (KJV)

That if thou shalt confess with thy mouth the Lord Jesus, and shalt believe in thine heart that God hath raised him from the dead, thou shalt be saved. For with the heart man believeth unto righteousness; and with the mouth confession is made unto salvation.

—Romans 10:9–10 (KJV)

Having predestinated us unto the adoption of children by Jesus Christ to himself, according to the good pleasure of his will, to the praise of the glory of his grace, wherein he hath made us accepted in the beloved. In whom we have redemption through his blood, the forgiveness of sins, according to the riches of his grace.

—Ephesians 1:5-7 (KJV)

New Testament Sacrifice

My little children, these things write I unto you, that ye sin not. And if any man sin, we have an advocate with the Father, Christ Jesus the righteous: And he is the propitiation for our sins: and not for ours only, but also for *the sins of* the whole world.

—1 John 2:1–2 (KJV)

For all have sinned, and come short of the glory of God.

—Romans 3:23

God, in his infinite wisdom and due to the separation from man, decided that Christ Jesus would be the only way to be reconcile back to God the Father. How stupid can people be? If there were another way to be reconciled with God, then Christ Jesus would not have had to die and be crucified for our sins. Don't be a fool. There is only one way to be reconciled back to God, and that is through Christ Jesus.

Jesus Is the Only Way to the Father

Jesus saith unto him, I am the way, the truth, and the life: no man cometh unto the Father, but by me. (John 14:6 KJV)

CHAPTER 5

Christians' Personal Accountability

To everything there is a season, and a time to every purpose under the heaven: a time to be born, and a time to die; a time to plant, and a time to pluck up that which is planted.

—Ecclesiastes 3:1–2 (KJV)

And why call ye me, Lord, Lord, and do not the things which I say?

—Luke 6:46 (KJV)

And Samuel said, Hath the LORD as great delight in burnt offerings and sacrifices, as in obeying the voice of the LORD? Behold, to obey is better than sacrifice, and to hearken than the fat of rams. For rebellion is as the sin of witchcraft, and stubbornness is as iniquity and idolatry. Because thou hast rejected the word of the LORD, he hath also rejected thee from being king. And Saul said unto Samuel, I have sinned: for I have transgressed the commandment of the LORD, and thy words: because I feared the people, and obeyed their voice.

—1 Samuel 15:22–24 (KJV)

Because of Saul's disobedience to God, he was rejected from being King Saul. He thought he would solve the problem of God's rejection by killing David and using witchcraft for guidance. Today so many people turn to other sources for guidance to fix their problems, such as tarot cards, Ouija boards, foretellers, and other false religions to solve their problems. You must fear and respect God more than you do people. Man's wrath is temporary. God's wrath is eternal. Some men and women's first concern is to please others and not the Lord. Disobedience to God's Word will cause us to sin and to suffer the wrath of God. Many people have suffered the wrath of God due to disobedience, just as King Saul did. If you don't recognize the Word of God as the authority in your life, you are destined to physical and spiritual failure.

> Wherefore gird up the loins of your mind, be sober, and hope to the end for the grace that is to be brought unto you at the revelation of Jesus Christ. (1 Peter 1:13 KJV)

> Go ye therefore, and teach all nations, baptizing them in the name of the Father, and of the Son, and of the Holy Ghost: Teaching them to observe all things whatsoever I have commanded you: and, lo, I am with you always, even unto the end of the world. Amen. (Matthew 28:19–20 KJV)

We must realize that we are eternal beings living in a temporary world for the purpose of choosing our eternal destination. While on earth, we have been given a season, purpose, and a time period to achieve our goals that the Lord has set before us. Our main goal is to accept Christ Jesus as our Lord and Savior. Next, we must reach out to make disciples of people for all have sinned and come short of the glory of God. We must obey his Word (Bible), love his people, deny self, and live our life according to the will of the Lord. We must use our spiritual gifts to reach the lost souls.

And God hath set some in the church, first apostles, secondarily prophets, thirdly teachers, after that miracles, then gifts of healings, helps, governments, diversities of tongues. (1 Corinthians 12:28–30 KJV)

And he gave some, apostles; and some, prophets; and some, evangelists; and some, pastors and teachers. (Ephesians 4:11 KJV)

Christ Jesus Expectation for Christian service

When the Son of man shall come in his glory, and all the holy angels with him, then shall he sit upon the throne of his glory: and before him shall be gathered all nations: and he shall separate them one from another, as a shepherd divideth his sheep from the goats: and he shall set the sheep on his right hand, but the goats on the left. Then shall the King say unto them on his right hand, Come, ye blessed of my Father, inherit the kingdom prepared for you from the foundation of the world: for I was an hungred, and ye gave me meat: I was thirsty, and ye gave me drink: I was a stranger, and ye took me in: naked, and ye clothed me: I was sick, and ye visited me: I was in prison, and ye came unto me. Then shall the righteous answer him, saying, Lord, when saw we thee an hungred, and fed thee? Or thirsty, and gave thee drink? When saw we thee a stranger, and took thee in? or naked, and clothed thee? Or when saw we thee sick, or in prison, and came unto thee? And the King shall answer and say unto them, Verily I say unto you, Inasmuch as ye have done it unto one of the least of these my brethren, ye have done it unto me. Then shall he say also unto them on the left hand, Depart from me, ye cursed, into everlasting fire, prepared for the devil and his angels: for I was an hungred, and ye gave me no meat: I was thirsty, and ye gave me no drink: I was a stranger, and ye took me not in: naked, and ye clothed me not: sick, and in prison, and ye visited me not. Then shall they also answer him, saying, Lord, when saw we thee an hungred, or athirst, or a stranger, or naked, or sick, or in prison, and did not minister unto thee? Then shall he answer them, saying, Verily I say unto you, Inasmuch as ye did it not to one of the least of these, ye did it not to me. And these shall go away into everlasting punishment: but the righteous into life eternal. (Matthews 25:31–46 KJV)

You are accountable for your time on earth. Don't be a Christian couch potato. Love is action. God gave his only begotten Son to save the souls of humanity. You must find your area of service in the body of Christ Jesus to work and use your gifts and talents to uplift the body of Christ. There are no excuses. We are in a spiritual war. You will go through trials and tribulations, but the salvation of Christ Jesus and the promises of heavenly rewards are worth enduring the fight to the end of your life.

CHAPTER 6

Spiritual Warfare and You

Churches Scenario
Pastors that Wound Their Members

> Woe be unto the pastors that destroy and scatter the sheep of my pasture saith the LORD. Therefore thus saith the LORD God of Israel against the pastors that feed my people; Ye have scattered my flock, and driven them away, and have not visited them: behold, I will visit upon you the evil of your doings, saith the LORD. (Jeremiah 23:1–2 (KJV)

Debra was a faithful member of forty-four years at her church. The Lord called her to be an Evangelist minister. She had already served as a missionary, Sunday school teacher, youth leader, and street outreach leader. Her pastor told her there was no room for her in the ministry. If Debra would have been a new Christian in Christ Jesus, this would have wounded her faith in the Lord. How was Debra able to overcome the rejection of her pastor? She remembered this scripture.

> Jesus says, I know thy works, and thy labour, and thy patience, and how thou canst not bear them which are evil: And hast borne, and hast

patience, and for my name's sake hast laboured, and hast not fainted. (Revelation 2:2a, 3)

As long as Christ Jesus knows my works and my labor, that's all that matters.

Driving Scenario

When driving and you attempt to change lanes, the person in the other lane most often will speed up to stop you from getting in front of them. Why? Because their hearts are full of evil and rebellious thoughts.

Work Scenario

Carrie was waiting on her new work badge to be sent to her from the corporate office. The expected arrive date to her job location was December 5. However, by December 20, Carrie still hadn't received her new work badge. She informed her manager, and he contacted the corporate office. Robert, at the corporate office, said he had sent it to Susan's office. Susan was on vacation, and her supervisor, Mitzi, found Carrie's work badge in Susan's desk drawer. Satan used Susan to intentionally hold up the delivery of Carrie work badge.

Family Issues, Moving Day

Ronald and Ryan were planning on helping their mother move today. Ronald and Ryan got into an argument. Ronald refused to help his mother move. Erica, the mother, and Ryan left without Ronald. Erica called Granny D and told her of the situation. Granny D called Ronald and Ryan on their cells phone and helped them to recognize this incident was spiritual warfare. They both agreed to work together and to help their mother move.

What cause these brothers' division?

The Video Game Stronghold

Richard is a twenty-one-year-old male. He quit his job when the baby was born to be with the baby's mother during labor and the birth of their newborn baby girl. Since the birth of his daughter, he did nothing but play video games. He was not looking for work to meet his financial obligation as a father. He was spiritually bound. The Word of God says if a man does not provider for his family is worse than an infidel. "But if any provide not for his own, and especially for those of his own house, he hath denied the faith, and is worse than an infidel. (1 Timothy 5:8 KJV)

An Infidel is one who is not a Christian and who opposes Christianity.

Home Scenario

The Bible says to honor your mother and father.

> Children, obey your parents in the Lord: for this is right. Honour thy father and mother; which is the first commandment with promise; that it may be well with thee, and thou mayest live long on the earth. And, ye fathers, provoke not your children to wrath: but bring them up in the nurture and admonition of the Lord. (Ephesians 6:1–4 KJV)

Valerie grew up with a very close relationship with her grandmother. She loved to go to church with her, sing in the choir, and participate in youth activities. When she turned sixteen, she stopped going to church and has had frequent arguments with her mother. She even stated that she wanted to hurt her mother and go live with her father. She has become very aggressive by fighting with others in school. Valerie felt she was grown and did not have to obey her mother. What changed Valerie attitude toward her mother?

Mental Challenges
Mental Illness

> Lord, have mercy on my son: for he is luna-
> tick, and sore vexed: for ofttimes he falleth into
> the fire, and oft into the water. And Jesus rebuked
> the devil; and he departed out of him: and the
> child was cured from that very hour. (Matthew
> 17:15, 18 KJV)

Mental illness is not always from heredity or a trauma. Demons or evil spirits can enter into unprotected souls, those who have not been covered by the blood of Christ Jesus due to their young age or those who have willfully chosen to reject Christ Jesus's salvation as the only way to God.

Demons love to enter physical bodies to control the thoughts and action of people. People who are possessed often hear voices and messages from the demons. Many horrific crimes have been committed by people who were possessed by demons. Satan and demons don't have a way back to God. They have no hope, and they seek to destroy humans for having the opportunity to reconcile with God through the blood of Christ Jesus.

The Battle Is in the Mind

> And be not conformed to this world: but
> be ye transformed by the renewing of your mind,
> that ye may prove what is that good, and accept-
> able, and perfect, will of God. (Romans 12:2
> KJV)

> For as he thinketh in his heart, so is he: Eat
> and drink, saith he to thee; but his heart is not
> with thee. (Proverbs 23:7 KJV)

The mind controls the body and thoughts of the soul. We have to guard are thoughts with the word of God. The mind is like a computer, nothing in and nothing out. We must use the Bible to feed our mind with the word of God. The Holy Spirit uses the mind to send messages to our thoughts for our direction, instruction, and correction. Satan, aka the devil, directs thoughts to our mind to kill, steal, and destroy us. We must learn to judge the thoughts we receive by the word of God.

Physical Challenges

> And he said unto me, My grace is sufficient for thee: for my strength is made perfect in weakness. (2 Corinthians 12:9 KJV)

Apostle Paul was afflicted with hip pain and endured constant physical illness with faith, patience, and trust in the Lord to help him complete his mission in life. He was an obedient and strong servant for Christ Jesus. Apostle Paul said, "Most gladly, therefore, will I rather glory in my infirmities that the power of Christ may rest upon me." Many people have physical challenges because of birth, accidents, or intentional harm inflected by others. We must face our issues knowing that Christ Jesus can heal, or that you must endure your physical afflictions. The will of God takes precedence over our wants or desire.

Relationship with Christ Jesus
Jesus Is Our True friend

> Ye are my friends, if ye do whatsoever I command you. (John 15:14 KJV)

> And why call ye me Lord, Lord and do not things that I say. (Luke 6:46 KJV)

Family Relationships

A. Relationship with spouse

> Let the husband render unto the wife due benevolence (respect): and likewise also the wife unto the husband. The wife hath not power of her own body, but the husband: and likewise also the husband hath not power of his own body, but the wife. Defraud (don't deprived) ye not one the other, except it be with consent for a time, that ye may give yourselves to fasting and prayer; and come together again, that Satan tempt you not for your incontinency. (1 Corinthians 7: 3–5 KJV)

Husband and wife must communicate with love, kindness, understanding, and be willing to serve with actions of love.

B. Relationships with children

> Children, obey your parents in the Lord: for this is right. Honour thy father and mother; which is the first commandment with promise; that it may be well with thee, and thou mayest live long on the earth. And, ye fathers, provoke not your children to wrath: but bring them up in the nurture and admonition of the Lord. (Ephesians 6:1–4 KJV)

God has given us order in the family, which is father, mother, and children. Children should obey and honor their parents. He also gives children blessing that it will be well with thee and live a long life on the earth. Children should be treated with patience, love, and respect. They should be trained to obey the Word of God, their parents, and others. Parents should be loving, patience, supportive, and use good judgment when correcting their children.

Work

> Servants, be obedient to them that are your masters according to the flesh, with fear and trembling, in singleness of your heart, as unto Christ; not with eyeservice, as men pleasers; but as the servants of Christ, doing the will of God from the heart; with good will doing service, as to the Lord, and not to men: knowing that whatsoever good thing any man doeth, the same shall he receive of the Lord, whether he be bond or free. (Ephesians 6:5–8 KJV)

Martha, the supervisor, asked Kay to type a work authorization for a home health agency. Kay typed the authorization. A couple days later, Martha deliberately changed the authorization to incorrect information. It caused other departments involved in the process to be stopped. When the error was brought to Debra's attention, she knew immediately that the authorization had been intentionally changed. Martha allowed the devil to manipulate her mind for evil deeds. Satan uses people to harm you and tear your character down.

Life after Death

> There was a certain rich man, which was clothed in purple and fine linen, and fared sumptuously every day: And there was a certain beggar named Lazarus, which was laid at his gate, full of sores, and desiring to be fed with the crumbs which fell from the rich man's table: moreover the dogs came and licked his sores. And it came to pass, that the beggar died, and was carried by the angels into Abraham's bosom: the rich man

also died, and was buried; And in hell he lift up his eyes, being in torments, and seeth Abraham afar off, and Lazarus in his bosom. And he cried and said, Father Abraham, have mercy on me, and send Lazarus, that he may dip the tip of his finger in water, and cool my tongue; for I am tormented in this flame. But Abraham said, Son, remember that thou in thy lifetime receivedst thy good things, and likewise Lazarus evil things: but now he is comforted, and thou art tormented. And beside all this, between us and you there is a great gulf fixed: so that they which would pass from hence to you cannot; neither can they pass to us, that *would come* from thence. Then he said, I pray thee therefore, father, that thou wouldest send him to my father's house: for I have five brethren; that he may testify unto them, lest they also come into this place of torment. Abraham saith unto him, they have Moses and the prophets; let them hear them. And he said, Nay, father Abraham: but if one went unto them from the dead, they will repent. And he said unto him, If they hear not Moses and the prophets, neither will they be persuaded, though one rose from the dead. (Luke 9:19–31 KJV)

We are eternal spiritual beings. Just like a caterpillar transform into a butterfly, we will also be transformed. We are born as a physical human being. Then at death, we detach from the physical body, and our spiritual body is releases.

In the above scriptures, you recognized the spiritual body has remembrance of the former physical life on earth. Lazarus and the rich man after death remembered and recognized each other. They were able to talk and to see each other. The rich man has feelings; he felt the flames of hell and wanted a drop of water from Lazarus. The rich man remembered his brothers on earth and wanted to go back to earth to tell them not to come to the burning hell. Abraham told him that they have Moses and the prophets. Christ Jesus, while on earth, preached more about hell than heaven because he does not want any soul to be lost.

CHAPTER 7

Christian Weapons for Spiritual Warfare

The Spiritual Battle

Finally, my brethren, be strong in the Lord, and in the power of his might. Put on the whole armour of God, that ye may be able to stand against the wiles of the devil. For we wrestle not against flesh and blood, but against principalities, against powers, against the rulers of the darkness of this world, against spiritual wickedness in high *places*. Wherefore take unto you the whole armour of God, that ye may be able to withstand in the evil day, and having done all, to stand. Stand therefore, having your loins girt about with truth, and having on the breastplate of righteousness; and your feet shod with the preparation of the gospel of peace; above all, taking the shield of faith, wherewith ye shall be able to quench all the fiery darts of the wicked. And take the helmet of salvation, and the sword of the Spirit, which is the word of God: praying always with all prayer and supplication in the Spirit, and

watching thereunto with all perseverance and
supplication for all saints.

—Ephesians 6:10–18 (KJV)

Disciples of Christ Jesus are in a spiritual war that also affects us physically and mentally. Multitudes of Christians are unaware that they are target practice for the devil and his demons because they don't know they are standing on a spirit battlefield. The Word of God says we perish for lack of knowledge. This lack of knowledge manifest in suicide, mental illness, physical abuse to others, and many more evil deeds and misfortune.

Casting Out Demons

And when he was come into the house, his
disciples asked him privately, Why could not we
cast him out? And he said unto them, This kind
can come forth by nothing, but by prayer and
fasting. (Mark 9:28–29 KJV)

Fighting against spiritual wickedness requires
fasting and praying. Fasting allow you to deny your-
self, so that you can receive spiritual power from
Christ Jesus by praying to him.

Spiritual Fast

But thou, when thou fastest, anoint thine
head, and wash thy face. (Matthew 6:17 KJV)

When you make a decision to go on a fast for one day or even a half a day on a spiritual fast which consist of just drinking water. Look normal when you go on a fast don't advertise the fast. The fast is between you and Christ Jesus. You will find that Satan will use people to bring you food in the morning and someone will want to buy you lunch. Satan will make many attempts to help you break your fast. Be wise and recognized the enemy attempts to break your fast.

When You Fail to Trust the Word of God

> Trust in the LORD with all thine heart; and lean not unto thine own understanding. In all thy ways acknowledge him, and he shall direct thy paths. (Proverbs 3:5–6 KJV)

Many people fail to call upon the Lord when going through trials and tribulations. In regards to your spouse, relationships, children, job, church, social clubs, siblings, or parental issues, many people make the wrong decision to solving their problems. They try drugs to solve their problems; making their problems worst; or they try friends and relationship to feel the void in their life. Ask the Lord for help in all of your needs and desires. He wants a relationship with you. The Lord said that his sheep know his voice. Do you know when the Lord is speaking to you? If you don't, read the Bible more and pray more. All of your thoughts can be measured by the word of God.

CHAPTER 8

⌘

Debra's Visions and Personal Experience from God

Age 16, Vision of Hell

I had a vision of hell at the age of sixteen. The Lord had me to fly over the lake of Fire. I saw multitudes of heads bobbing under the lava. Then he took me to heaven, the door opened, and I woke up from my vision.

Age 24, Demons Family Attack

As a child, Sally loved to play with the Ouija board. The Ouija board moved and answered Sally's questions. In 1979, my cousin Sally, with her mother, Pauline, and myself went to an evening church revival with Sally and Aunt Betty. During the service, the pastor called for people to line up for prayer. When Sally was touched by the pastor, Sally's body went into a violent shaking on the floor with screams coming from her body, and her eyes were closed. The church leaders' prayed many hours. Finally, they were able to stand her up with her eyes still closed. They put a Bible over her heart, and then loud screams came from her body.

Finally, Sally opened her eyes and became conscious. On the way home, I asked Sally, "Where were you when the demons were controlling your body?" She said she was pushed back in her mind and could not get out. She said it felt like someone was sticking knives in her body. I told her that's when they put the Bible over your heart.

After that night, about two weeks went by. Then one night, when I had gone to a summer school teacher meeting for my children, when I got home, I saw a fire burning in Sally's mom's (Pauline) yard because we lived next door to them. I took my children home and left them with my husband. I went next door to tell Pauline a fire was burning in her yard.

When I entered into her home, other people were there whom I did not know. She introduced Brother Jose and another man, along with Aunt Betty and Sally. Pauline said, "We are conducting an exorcist with Brother Jose." Brother Jose asked me if I was a Christian, I replied yes. He said, "If you like, you can stay for the exorcist, but you must pray."

Brother Jose began to pray, and Sally fell out on the floor. Her body began to shake and flip-flop like a large fish. She was spitting up fluid from her body. Brother Jose asked the demons, "What are you planning on doing with Sally?" In a deep male voice, they said they were going to kill her in a car accident.

He then asked, "How many demons are in Sally?" The demons replied legions. Then Brother Jose said in a loud authoritative voice, "In the name of Christ Jesus, I command you to come out of Sally." We who were present in the room went into strong prayer in the name of Christ Jesus, commanding the demons to leave Sally's body. After some time, Sally's body stopped shaking, and there was a calm, and Sally woke up from the stronghold the demons had put on her. The whole family from the west coast to the east coast was rejoicing over Sally's deliverance from Satan's stronghold.

About two weeks after the exorcist, about noon, I picked my children up from summer school. I told them to take a nap. I laid down in my bedroom to also take a nap. About ten minutes went by, I felt an invisible spirit jumped on me, I was unable to move, and it felt like someone was squeezing my brain. I thought I was having a stroke, and then my daughter, Yvette came in my room to tell on her sister, Erica, and then the paralyzing and squeezing feeling stop. I dismissed the incident.

About another week went by, after I had picked up the children from summer school, during nap time, another invisible spirit jumped on me. I was unable to move again for about two hours, then the stronghold stop. I discussed the issue with my mother and grandmother, and they told me to call on the name of Christ Jesus. I made up my mind no demon in hell was going to drive me crazy.

Another week went by and after nap time again, the invisible spirit (demon) jumped on me again. I could not verbally speak, but in my mind, I got angry and bold, and I said like "Christ Jesus defeated you on the cross, and through his shed blood, I defeated you also. In the name of Christ Jesus, Satan and demons, you got to go." Since that time, I have not had any more demonic attacks.

I have been able to share my story with many other people who had similar experiences but did not know it was a demonic attack.

Age 25, My Spirit Separated Itself from My Physical Body

In March of 1980, I was working as a nurse assistant. I had taken the job assignment of a sitter at Brotman Hospital in Culver City. I had one comatose patient. I started my shift at 11:00 p.m. I had checked the patient and took his vital signs. I started reading a book, and about 11:45 p.m., my spirit lifted up out of my body, and my spirit was up on the ceiling of the room. I could see myself sitting in the chair, holding the book, and the patient lying in the hospital bed. In my mind, I asked the Lord, "Lord, am I going to die?" Then my spirit went back into my body. I can remember that experience like it was yesterday. I will never forget that experience. I would like you to know that I have never ever tried any illegal drugs in my life. I know without a doubt that my soul can only be saved by the name of Christ Jesus.

Age 62, Vision of Hell

About two weeks after my brother, Marvin, died on June 8, 2016, I had a vision dream. I met my brother, and I said, "Marvin, you made it [heaven]."

He said, "Yes, I made it." He said people tried to trick him. He said he had a tiny apartment in heaven. Marvin had lived a homosexual lifestyle. However, in June of 2015, he repented of his homosexual lifestyle and surrendered to the Word of God.

I looked around and said, "Marvin, who are all these thousands of people standing in line?"

Marvin said, "I don't know. He said let's walk to the front of the line." We walked to front of the line. We saw two demons putting a lady in the lake of fire. She screamed the most awful scream that I have ever heard.

Then I said, "Why don't the other people run?"

The Holy Spirit said, "They can't run. They had been judged by the Word of God."

CHAPTER 9

Before The Rapture

Before the Rapture

But of that day and hour knoweth no man,
no, not the angels of heaven, but my Father only.
—Matthew 24:36 (KJV)

But I would not have you to be ignorant,
brethren, concerning them which are asleep,
that ye sorrow not, even as others which have no
hope. For if we believe that Jesus died and rose
again, even so them also which sleep in Jesus will
God bring with him. For this we say unto you by
the word of the Lord, that we which are alive and
remain unto the coming of the Lord shall not
prevent them which are asleep. For the Lord himself shall descend from heaven with a shout, with
the voice of the archangel, and with the trump of
God: and the dead in Christ shall rise first: Then
we which are alive and remain shall be caught up
together with them in the clouds, to meet the
Lord in the air: and so shall we ever be with the
Lord. Wherefore comfort one another with these
words.

—1 Thessalonians 4:13–18 (KJV)

Christ Jesus departed from this earth by ascension to heaven over two thousand years ago. Christ Jesus is coming back to take his bride, the church which are the true Christian believers. Many will be left behind to suffer the tribulation period.

The History of the Three Temple Capitals of Jerusalem in the Bible

The First Jerusalem Temple of God

The crowning achievement of King Solomon's reign was the erection of the magnificent temple (Hebrew, *Beit haMikdash*) in the capital city of ancient Israel, Jerusalem. Solomon spared no expense for the building's creation. He ordered vast quantities of cedarwood from King Hiram of Tyre (1 Kings 5).

The Second Jerusalem Temple of God

The Second Temple was the Jewish holy temple which stood on the Temple Mount in Jerusalem during the Second Temple period, between 516 BCE and 70 CE. According to Jewish tradition, it replaced Solomon's Temple (the First Temple), which was destroyed by the Babylonians in 586 BCE when Jerusalem was conquered, and part of the population of the kingdom of Judah was taken into exile to Babylon.

The Second Temple was built on the same site (Ezra 1:1–4). Sacrifices to God were once again resumed. During the first century BCE, Herod, the Roman appointed head of Judea, made substantial modifications to the temple and the surrounding mountain, enlarging and expanding the temple. The Second Temple, however, met the same fate as the first and was destroyed by the Romans in 70 CE, following the failure of the Great Revolt. Jewish eschatology includes a belief that the Second Temple will be replaced by a future Third Temple.

The Third Jerusalem Temple of God

December 5, 2017, President Donald Trump declared that he would recognize the city of Jerusalem as the capital of Israel. The United States embassy in Israel is now located the city of Tel Aviv but will be moved to city of Jerusalem in the near future. On May 14, 2018, the United States embassy of Tel Aviv was moved to Jerusalem. The Antichrist will dwell in the capital of Jerusalem. This is the third temple.

CHAPTER 10

The Rapture

The Rapture

Behold, he cometh with clouds; and every eye shall see him, and they *also* which pierced him: and all kindreds of the earth shall wail because of him. Even so, Amen.
—Revelation 1:7 (KJV)

And to you who are troubled rest with us, when the Lord Jesus shall be revealed from heaven with his mighty angels, In flaming fire taking vengeance on them that know not God, and that obey not the gospel of our Lord Jesus Christ: who shall be punished with everlasting destruction from the presence of the Lord, and from the glory of his power; when he shall come to be glorified in his saints, and to be admired in all them that believe (because our testimony among you was believed) in that day.
—2 Thessalonians 1:7–10 (KJV)

CHAPTER 11

The Tribulation Period

For then shall be great tribulation, such as was not since the beginning of the world to this time, no, nor ever shall be. And except those days should be shortened, there should no flesh be saved: but for the elect's sake those days shall be shortened. Then if any man shall say unto you, Lo, here *is* Christ, or there; believe *it* not. For there shall arise false Christs, and false prophets, and shall shew great signs and wonders; insomuch that, if *it were* possible, they shall deceive the very elect.

—Matthew 24:21–24 (KJV)

But take ye heed: behold, I have foretold you all things. But in those days, after that tribulation, the sun shall be darkened, and the moon shall not give her light, and the stars of heaven shall fall, and the powers that are in heaven shall be shaken. And then shall they see the Son of man coming in the clouds with great power and glory. And then shall he send his angels, and shall gather together his elect from the four winds, from the uttermost part of the earth to the uttermost part of heaven. Now learn a parable of the fig tree; When her branch is yet tender, and put-teth forth leaves, ye know that summer is near: so ye in like manner, when ye shall see these things come to pass, know that it is nigh, *even* at the doors. Verily I say unto you, that this genera-tion shall not pass, till all these things be done. Heaven and earth shall pass away: but my words shall not pass away.

—Mark 13:23–31 (KJV)

And he (Devil) causeth all, both small and great, rich and poor, free and bond, to receive a mark in their right hand, or in their foreheads: and that no man might buy or sell, save he that had the mark, or the name of the beast, or the number of his name. Here is wisdom. Let him that hath understanding count the number of the beast: for it is the number of a man; and his num-ber is Six hundred threescore and six.

—Revelation 13:16–18 (KJV)

And the third angel followed them, say-ing with a loud voice, If any man worship the beast and his image, and receive his mark in his forehead, or in his hand, the same shall drink of the wine of the wrath of God, which is poured out without mixture into the cup of his indig-nation; and he shall be tormented with fire and brimstone in the presence of the holy angels, and in the presence of the Lamb: and the smoke of their torment ascendeth up for ever and ever: and they have no rest day nor night, who worship the beast and his image, and whosoever receiveth the mark of his name.

—Revelation 14:9–11

If you accept the mark of the beast on the forehead or hand, there is no forgiveness you. You are condemned to the lake of fire.

Martyr Souls in the Tribulation Period

And when he had opened the fifth seal, I saw under the altar the souls of them that were slain for the word of God, and for the testimony which they held: and they cried with a loud voice, saying, How long, O Lord, holy and true, dost thou not judge and avenge our blood on them that dwell on the earth? And white robes were given unto every one of them; and it was said unto them, that they should rest yet for a little season, until their fellow servants also and their brethren, that should be killed as they were, should be fulfilled. (Revelation 6:9–11 KJV)

And one of the elders answered, saying unto me, What are these which are arrayed in white robes? And whence came they? And I said unto him, Sir, thou knowest. And he said to me, These are they which came out of great tribulation, and have washed their robes, and made them white in the blood of the Lamb. Therefore are they before the throne of God, and serve him day and night in his temple: and he that sitteth on the throne shall dwell among them. They shall hunger no more, neither thirst any more; neither shall the sun light on them, nor any heat. For the Lamb which is in the midst of the throne shall feed them, and shall lead them unto living fountains of waters: and God shall wipe away all tears from their eyes. (Revelation 7:13–17 KJV)

And I saw thrones, and they sat upon them, and judgment was given unto them: and I saw the souls of them that were beheaded for the witness of Jesus, and for the word of God, and which had not worshipped the beast, neither his image, neither had received his mark upon their foreheads, or in their hands; and they lived and reigned with Christ a thousand years. (Revelation 20:4 KJV)

CHAPTER 12

Christ's Thousand-Year Reign

And I saw heaven opened, and behold a white horse; and he that sat upon him was called Faithful and True, and in righteousness he doth judge and make war. His eyes were as a flame of fire, and on his head were many crowns; and he had a name written, that no man knew, but he himself. And he was clothed with a vesture dipped in blood: and his name is called The Word of God. And the armies which were in heaven followed him upon white horses, clothed in fine linen, white and clean. And out of his mouth goeth a sharp sword, that with it he should smite the nations: and he shall rule them with a rod of iron: and he treadeth the winepress of the fierceness and wrath of Almighty God. And he hath on his vesture and on his thigh a name written, KING OF KINGS, AND LORD OF LORDS. And I saw an angel standing in the sun; and he cried with a loud voice, saying to all the fowls that fly in the midst of heaven, Come and gather yourselves together unto the supper of the great God; that ye may eat the flesh of kings, and the flesh of captains, and the flesh of mighty men, and the flesh of horses, and of them that sit on them, and the flesh of all men, both free and bond, both small and great. And I saw the beast, and the kings of the earth, and their armies, gathered together to make war against him that sat on the horse, and against his army. And the beast was taken, and with him the false prophet that wrought miracles before him, with which he deceived them that had received the mark of the beast, and them that worshipped his image. These both were cast alive into a lake of fire burning with brimstone.

—Revelation 19:11–20

And I saw an angel come down from heaven, having the key of the bottomless pit and a great chain in his hand. And he laid hold on the dragon, that old serpent, which is the Devil, and Satan, and bound him a thousand years, and cast him into the bottomless pit, and shut him up, and set a seal upon him, that he should deceive the nations no more, till the thousand years should be fulfilled: and after that he must be loosed a little season. And I saw thrones, and they sat upon them, and judgment was given unto them: and *I saw* the souls of them that were beheaded for the witness of Jesus, and for the word of God, and which had not worshipped the beast, neither his image, neither had received *his* mark upon their foreheads, or in their hands; and they lived and reigned with Christ a thousand years. But the rest of the dead lived not again until the thousand years were finished. This is the first resurrection. Blessed and holy *is* he that hath part in the first resurrection: on such the second death hath no power, but they shall be priests of God and of Christ, and shall reign with him a thousand years.

—Revelation 20:1–6 (KJV)

CHAPTER 13

After the Thousand-Year Reign

And when the thousand years are expired, Satan shall be loosed out of his prison, and shall go out to deceive the nations, which are in the four quarters of the earth, Gog and Magog, to gather them together to battle: the number of whom *is* as the sand of the sea. And they went up on the breadth of the earth, and compassed the camp of the saints about, and the beloved city: and fire came down from God out of heaven, and devoured them. And the devil that deceived them was cast into the lake of fire and brimstone, where the beast and the false prophet *are*, and shall be tormented day and night forever and ever.

—Revelation 20:7–10 (KJV)

The devil is a loser. He does not have a way back to God. He refuses to acknowledge that he is a creation and not a creator. The devil will be allowed to tempt the people after the thousand-year reign that had not been tempted by him (sin) so that they will have to choose between accepting Christ Jesus or rejecting him as Lord and Savior.

CHAPTER 14

The Great White Throne

And I saw a great white throne, and him that sat on it, from whose face the earth and the heaven fled away; and there was found no place for them. And I saw the dead, small and great, stand before God; and the books were opened: and another book was opened, which is *the book* of life: and the dead were judged out of those things which were written in the books, according to their works. And the sea gave up the dead which were in it; and death and hell delivered up the dead which were in them: and they were judged every man according to their works. And death and hell were cast into the lake of fire. This is the second death. And whosoever was not found written in the book of life was cast into the lake of fire.

—Revelation 20:11–15 (KJV)

But the fearful, and unbelieving, and the abominable, and murderers, and whoremongers, and sorcerers, and idolaters, and all liars, shall have their part in the lake which burneth with fire and brimstone: which is the second death.

—Revelation 21:8

CHAPTER 15

Eternity with Christ Jesus

For God created man to be immortal, and made him to be an image of his own eternity.
—Wisdom of Solomon 2:23 (KJV)

Let not your heart be troubled: ye believe in God, believe also in me. In my Father's house are many mansions: if *it were* not *so*, I would have told you. I go to prepare a place for you. And if I go and prepare a place for you, I will come again, and receive you unto myself; that where I am, *there* ye may be also. And whither I go ye know, and the way ye know. Thomas saith unto him, Lord, we know not whither thou goest; and how can we know the way? Jesus saith unto him, I am the way, the truth, and the life: no man cometh unto the Father, but by me.
—John 14:1–6 (KJV)

And I saw a new heaven and a new earth: for the first heaven and the first earth were passed away; and there was no more sea. And I John saw the holy city, new Jerusalem, coming down from God out of heaven, prepared as a bride adorned for her husband. And I heard a great voice out of heaven saying, Behold, the tabernacle of God *is* with men, and he will dwell with them, and they shall be his people, and God himself shall be with them, *and be* their God. And God shall wipe away all tears from their eyes; and there shall be no more death, neither sorrow, nor crying, neither shall there be any more pain: for the former things are passed away. And he that sat upon the throne said, Behold, I make all things new. And he said unto me, Write: for these words are true and faithful.

—Revelation 21:1–5 (KJV)

And he said unto me, It is done. I am Alpha and Omega, the beginning and the end. I will give unto him that is athirst of the fountain of the water of life freely. He that overcometh shall inherit all things; and I will be his God, and he shall be my son.

—Revelation 21:6–7

Behold, I come quickly: blessed *is* he that keepeth the sayings of the prophecy of this book. And, behold, I come quickly; and my reward *is* with me, to give every man according as his work shall be. I am Alpha and Omega, the beginning and the end, the first and the last. Blessed *are* they that do his commandments, that they may have right to the tree of life, and may enter in through the gates into the city.

—Revelation 22:12–14 (KJV)

[9]But as it is written, Eye hath not seen, nor ear heard, neither have entered into the heart of man, the things which God hath prepared for them that love him.

1 Corinthians 2:9 (KJV)

CONCLUSION

Eternity with the Trinity of God, God the Father (Yahweh), God the Son (Yeshua, Christ Jesus), and the Holy Spirit is better than burning in an eternal lake of fire.

SPIRITUAL WARFARE QUIZ

1. Have you ever looked at a person whom you didn't know and said I hate you?
2. Have you ever lied to someone just because you could?
3. Do you have a lot of anger in your heart toward family, friends, or strangers?
4. Does your mind allow strange and bad thoughts to constantly fill your mind?
5. Have your ever hurt a harmless animal for no reason?
6. Do you obey and apply the word of God to your life?
7. Do you have a personal relationship with Christ Jesus? If not, then why not?
8. Have you ever desire to kill someone?
9. Do you make stealing a way of life?
10. Is Christ Jesus really first in your life?
11. Do you find it hard to forgive people?
12. Do you believe in your heart that Christ Jesus is your personal Lord and Savior?

The author was inspired through the Holy Spirit and the Word of God the Bible (KJV) to recognize mankind's daily battle in spiritual warfare between Christ Jesus (good) versus Satan (evil). It is my goal to help people to recognize spiritual warfare in different areas of their lives, how to trust the word, believe the word and pray with expectations, and how to use Christian weapons to be victorious in personal battle.

REFERENCES

Christ Jesus
The Holy Spirit
King James Bible

ABOUT THE AUTHOR

 I am Debra Kay Houston Wong, an Evangelist minister and a true servant of Christ Jesus. My mission in life is to praise, worship, and obey to the Word of God. I began my walk in Christ Jesus in a Christian Baptist family upbringing with my grandmother, Carrie Mae Walker Dukes, my mother, Mary Larkin Houston, and my father, Woodrow Wilson Houston.

I accepted Christ Jesus as my Lord and Savior at the age of nine years old and was baptized like Christ Jesus in total water submersion at Macedonia Baptist Church on March 1964 in Los Angeles, California. I completed a two-year Bible study with Bible prophecy by mail. I raised my three children, Gregory Wong Jr., Erica Wong Simms Subramanian, and Yvette Wong, and two grandchildren, Ronald Simms III and Ryan Simms, in the Word of God as Christians. I graduated in 2015 from Southern California School of Ministry in Inglewood, California.

My Christian lifework has been an adult and children Sunday school teacher for over forty years, a Church missionary leader for adults and youth groups for over twenty years, and a street outreach organizer for years at three different churches. I am a LVN case manager, a computer trainer, and an Evangelist minister directly called by Christ Jesus.

CPSIA information can be obtained
at www.ICGtesting.com
Printed in the USA
BVHW031409050521
606414BV00011B/739

SPIRITUAL WARFARE AND YOU

INSPIRED BY CHRIST JESUS AND THE HOLY SPIRIT

The author was inspired through the Holy Spirit and the Word of God the Bible (KJV) to recognize mankind's daily battle in spiritual warfare between Christ Jesus (good) versus Satan (evil). It is the author's goal to help people to recognize spiritual warfare in different areas of their lives, how to trust the word, believe the Word and pray with expectation, and how to use fasting and prayer as Christian weapons to be victorious in personal battle.

Christian Faith
PUBLISHING

$12.95

ISBN 978-1-0980-7816-4

51295

9 781098 078164